IT'S MY STATE!

OREGON

Joyce Hart

Jacqueline Laks Gorman

Marshall Cavendish
Benchmark
New York

Published by Marshall Cavendish Benchmark
An imprint of Marshall Cavendish Corporation

Website: www.marshallcavendish.us

This publication represents the opinions and views of the authors based on their personal experience, knowledge, and research. The information in this book serves as a general guide only. The authors and publisher have used their best efforts in preparing this book and disclaim liability rising directly and indirectly from the use and application of this book.

Other Marshall Cavendish Offices:
Marshall Cavendish International (Asia) Private Limited, 1 New Industrial Road, Singapore 536196 • Marshall Cavendish International (Thailand) Co Ltd. 253 Asoke, 12th Flr, Sukhumvit 21 Road, Klongtoey Nua, Wattana, Bangkok 10110, Thailand • Marshall Cavendish (Malaysia) Sdn Bhd, Times Subang, Lot 46, Subang Hi-Tech Industrial Park, Batu Tiga, 40000 Shah Alam, Selangor Darul Ehsan, Malaysia

Marshall Cavendish is a trademark of Times Publishing Limited

All websites were available and accurate when this book was sent to press.

Library of Congress Cataloging-in-Publication Data
Hart, Joyce, 1954-
        Oregon / Joyce Hart and Jacqueline Laks Gorman.—2nd ed.
            p. cm. — (It's my state!)
        Summary: "Surveys the history, geography, government, economy, and people
        of Oregon"—Provided by publisher.
        Includes bibliographical references and index.
        ISBN 978-1-60870-525-2 (print) — ISBN 978-1-60870-703-4 (ebook)
        1. Oregon--Juvenile literature. I. Gorman, Jacqueline Laks, 1955-
        II. Title.
    F876.3.H37 2012
    979.5—dc22   2010044335

Second Edition developed for Marshall Cavendish Benchmark by RJF Publishing LLC (www.RJFpublishing.com)
Series Designer, Second Edition: Tammy West/Westgraphix LLC
Editor, Second Edition: Amanda Hudson

All maps, illustrations, and graphics © Marshall Cavendish Corporation. Maps and artwork on pages 6, 30, 31, 75, 76, and back cover by Christopher Santoro. Map and graphics on pages 8 and 48 by Westgraphix LLC.

The photographs in this book are used by permission and through the courtesy of:
Front cover: Gunter Max/WC/Alamy and Yellow Dog Productions/Getty Images (inset).
Alamy: Peter Arnold, Inc., 4 (left); D. Hurst, 4 (right), 51; Bruce Coleman Inc., 5 (left); Greg Vaughn, 17, 26, 40; Corbis RF, 20 (right); William Leaman, 20 (left); Mark Conlin, 21; Chuck Pefley, 22; North Wind Picture Archives, 24, 35, 36, ; Denis Frates, 29, 50; Danita Delimont, 38; Michele and Tom Grimm, 43; Rich Iwasaki, 52; IIene MacDonald, 54, 56; FogStock, 58; Andre Jenny, 60; AGStockUSA, 67; Kevin Schafer, 71 (left); Sharpencolour, 71 (right); Russ Bishop, 73.. **Getty Images:** Peter Lilja, 5 (right); Marc Muench, 9; Shanna Baker, 10; Panoramic Images, 12; Randy Wells, 13; Terry Donnelly, 14; Jonathan Kingston, 16; Jim and Jamie Dutcher, 18; Time & Life Pictures, 33; Getty Images, 34, 42, 46, 47 (left); Gerry Ellis, 37; WireImage, 47 (right); John Giustina, 48; Steve Satushek, 49; National Geographic, 65; Bruce Forster, 66; Cavan Images, 70; Scott Markewitz, 74. **Oregon Historical Society OrHi93065:** 25. **Oregon Zoo:** Michael Durham, 53. **Superstock:** George Ostertag, 11, 62; Stock Connection, 68; Age Fotostock, 69.

Printed in Malaysia (T).
135642

CONTENTS

State Tree: Douglas Fir

The Douglas fir, which can reach heights of over 300 feet (90 meters) and grows as straight as an arrow in Oregon's forests, was selected as the state tree in 1939. This evergreen tree was named for David Douglas, a botanist from Scotland who came to the United States to study plants in the 1820s. Because of its strength, wood from the Douglas fir is often used in constructing houses. The wood is said to be as sturdy as concrete.

State Fruit: Pear

In 2005, the Oregon legislature made the pear the state fruit. Pears are one of Oregon's most important crops. Oregon orchards grow a variety of pears, including Bosc, Bartlett, and Anjou. These tasty fruits are shipped throughout the country and around the world.

State Flower: Oregon Grape

In 1899, the legislature adopted the Oregon grape as the state flower. The Oregon grape plant is an evergreen bush that produces small bell-shaped yellow flowers in the spring and blue berries in the fall. The berries are not actually grapes, but they are edible when fully ripe. The Oregon grape is found all over the state, but most commonly along the Pacific Coast.

State Insect: Oregon Swallowtail Butterfly

Swallowtail butterflies are common on the East Coast, but the only kind that lives in the Pacific Northwest is the Oregon swallowtail. This black-and-yellow butterfly has a wingspan of 2.5 inches (6.4 centimeters) to 4 inches (10 cm). It prefers dry weather, so the best place to look for the Oregon swallowtail is east of the Cascade Mountains, especially along the cliffs of the Columbia River.

State Bird: Western Meadowlark

In 1927, Oregon schoolchildren voted in a poll to make the western meadowlark the state bird. The western meadowlark is recognized by its bright yellow chest and black V-shaped collar. This bird is only about 9 inches (23 cm) long. Its unique song sounds like someone playing a flute from a high note down to a low note. The meadowlark spends a great deal of time on the ground. When it does fly, it flaps its wings several times, then sails for a few seconds with its wings held still.

State Animal: Beaver

The beaver was almost completely wiped out in Oregon's woodlands by fur trappers. Today, the beaver is protected by state law, and beavers can again be found along many of Oregon's rivers. These animals are often called nature's engineers because of their ability to build complex dams that help to protect riverbanks from erosion. The beaver is also Oregon State University's mascot.

OREGON

Astoria

PACIFIC OCEAN

STATE OF OREGON 1859

Mount Hood

The Dalles

COLUMBIA RIVER

Milton-Freewater

HELLS CANYON NATIONAL RECREATION AREA

Portland

DESCHUTES RIVER

JOHN DAY RIVER

Pendleton

BLUE MOUNTAINS

La Grande

WALLOWA MOUNTAINS

SNAKE RIVER

Salem

CASCADE MOUNTAINS

WILLAMETTE NATIONAL FOREST

UMATILLA NATIONAL FOREST

Baker City

Albany

WILLAMETTE RIVER

DESCHUTES NATIONAL FOREST

Bend

Redmond

Ontario

Corvallis

Eugene

UMPQUA RIVER

NEWBERRY NATIONAL VOLCANIC MONUMENT

Burns

HARNEY LAKE

MALHEUR LAKE

LAKE OWYHEE

Coos Bay

COASTAL RANGE

Roseburg

CRATER LAKE

Alkali Lake

OWYHEE RIVER

Jordan Valley

ROGUE RIVER

FREMONT NATIONAL FOREST

SISKIYOU NATIONAL FOREST

UPPER KLAMATH LAKE

Brookings

Grants Pass

Medford

Klamath Falls

Lakeview

HART MOUNTAIN NATIONAL ANTELOPE REFUGE

N
W   E
S

The Beaver State

With a land area of 95,997 square miles (248,631 square kilometers), Oregon is a large state. In land area, it is the tenth-largest state in the nation. People who live in Oregon enjoy a wide variety of natural regions. The state has rain forests, hot and dry deserts, sandy beaches, and mountains topped with ice and snow. In between Oregon's two major mountain ranges, the Coast Range and the Cascade Mountains, is a large green valley. Called the Willamette Valley, it is where most Oregonians make their homes.

Oregon is divided into thirty-six counties. The state is rectangular in shape. From west to east, it is about 400 miles (650 km) wide, and from north to south, it is around 250 miles (400 km) long. If you were to begin a trip at Oregon's western shoreline, starting about midway down the coast, you would first travel across the Coast Range mountains.

Moving eastward, you would wander through the wide, green Willamette Valley before climbing the highest elevations in the state at the Cascade Mountains. At the eastern side of the Cascades, the climate turns very dry. The landscape changes from thick forests to mostly open plains. A major portion of the eastern part of the state is home

Quick Facts

OREGON BORDERS

North	Washington
South	California
	Nevada
East	Idaho
West	Pacific Ocean

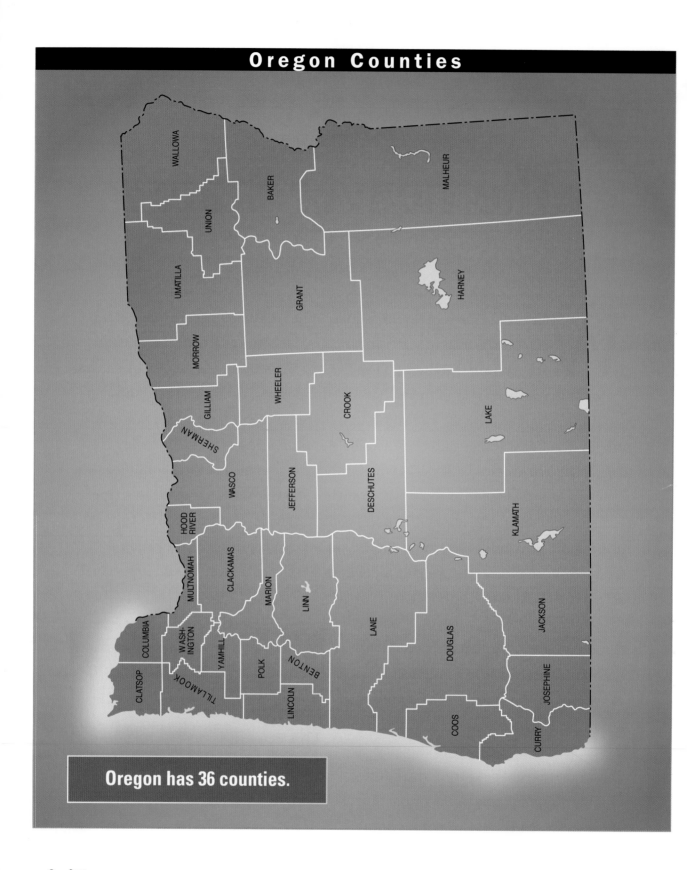

Oregon Counties

WALLOWA

BAKER

MALHEUR

UNION

HARNEY

UMATILLA

GRANT

MORROW

WHEELER

CROOK

LAKE

GILLIAM

SHERMAN

WASCO

JEFFERSON

DESCHUTES

KLAMATH

HOOD RIVER

MULTNOMAH

CLACKAMAS

MARION

LINN

LANE

DOUGLAS

JACKSON

COLUMBIA

WASH-
INGTON

YAMHILL

POLK

BENTON

JOSEPHINE

CLATSOP

TILLAMOOK

LINCOLN

COOS

CURRY

Oregon has 36 counties.

to many large farms. Near the eastern border of the state is the Blue Mountains range, a place where gold was once mined.

Natural Forces

Some of Oregon's major land formations began to take shape about 200 million years ago as the North American continent and the floor of the Pacific Ocean started bumping into one another. Earth's surface is made up of an outer layer about 60 miles (100 km) thick that is broken into many pieces, called plates. These plates move very slowly—some only 2 inches (5 cm) each year. When two plates bump into each other, one plate sometimes slides under the other. This is what happened to create the terrain that is now Oregon's western shore. The ocean plate sank under the coastline, and the land on the coast was pushed upward. This created the Coast Range mountains.

Mount Hood, which overlooks Lost Lake, is part of the Cascade Mountains.

As the ocean plate moved under the continent, the rock material that made up the plate became very hot and melted, turning into magma. This liquid rock eventually rushed to the surface. Magma released onto Earth's surface is called lava. After many explosions of lava, a line of volcanoes was created. These old and now mostly inactive volcanoes make up Oregon's Cascade Mountains.

Weather helped to create some of Oregon's other physical features. Moist air, blowing from the ocean, released heavy rainfall on the western slopes of the Coast Range and the Cascades. Water flowing down the mountainsides created rivers. These rivers fed the land and helped to produce a thick growth of trees and smaller plants. By the time the air moved past the top of the Cascades to the eastern side of the state, it was drained of moisture, so it blew hot and dry. This is why eastern Oregon has dry, desert-like climate conditions.

The Western Coast

The western boundary of Oregon is one of the most scenic shorelines in the world. In some places, the Coast Range mountains rise straight up from the Pacific Ocean. In other places along the coast, there are sandy beaches. More than twenty-two rivers flow out of the Coast Range and into the ocean, creating estuaries, which are the mouths of rivers where they meet the ocean. In these

Quick Facts

SEA LION CAVES

The largest sea caves in the world are found in Oregon, just north of Florence. About two hundred Northern sea lions (also called Stellar sea lions) live in the caves, which are the only known home for this species on the North American mainland.

estuaries, a wide range of wildlife can be found. The Columbia River estuary is the largest estuary in the region. It is located at the northernmost point of Oregon's ocean coast, on the border with Washington. In the middle of the Coast Range mountains is Siuslaw National Forest, which is a large rain forest.

There are small towns along the coast, such as Astoria, in the north. Florence, with its long sandy beaches, is a popular tourist town located at the middle of the coast. At the southern end of Oregon's ocean shoreline is Brookings. It is located in what is sometimes referred to as the Banana Belt of Oregon because of its mild weather.

The Willamette Valley

The Willamette Valley lies between the Coast Range, to the west, and the Cascade Mountains, to the east. At the northern end of the valley are Portland—the state's largest city—and the much-smaller Oregon City. At the southern end of the valley is Eugene, another of the state's major cities. The Willamette River flows from south to north through the valley.

When pioneers first crossed the high Cascade Mountains and entered the Willamette Valley, many of them thought they had reached a garden paradise. The valley looked like a great place to make a home, with its forests—an excellent source of lumber—and its many wild fruit-bearing bushes. The soil was very fertile, which meant it was good for growing crops, and the weather was

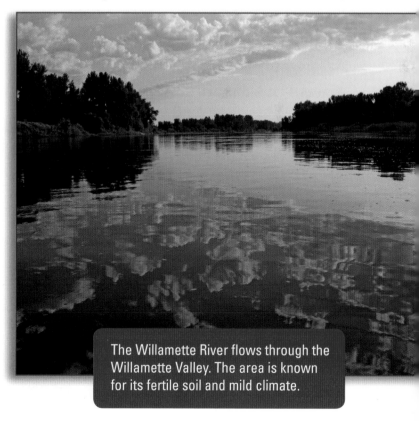

The Willamette River flows through the Willamette Valley. The area is known for its fertile soil and mild climate.

mild. Many different crops are now grown in the Willamette Valley, including mint, grass seeds, pumpkins, and corn. Today, more than 2 million Oregonians live in the Willamette Valley. Other cities in the region include Corvallis and Salem, the state capital.

The Cascade Mountains

Oregon's highest elevations are found in the Cascade Mountains. The state's highest point is the summit of Mount Hood, located east of Portland. Mount Hood is 11,239 feet (3,426 m) high. Other giant peaks in the Cascades include Mount Jefferson and the triple peaks of the Three Sisters. These large mountains are snow-capped year round. The Cascades stretch from northern California to British Columbia in Canada and contain more than a dozen active volcanoes (including Mount St. Helens in Washington). Eruptions in Oregon, however, are infrequent. The last eruption occurred on Mount Hood over two hundred years ago.

Mount Hood's summit is the highest point in Oregon.

Crater Lake is the deepest lake in the United States. The area around the lake receives more snowfall than any other part of Oregon.

Crater Lake, located in the southern-Oregon Cascades, was created when an ancient volcano, called Mount Mazama, exploded and then collapsed. This eruption created a deep depression, or hole, that eventually filled with water. The lake is almost 2,000 feet (600 m) deep. It is the deepest lake in the United States and the seventh-deepest lake in the world. In the winter, the area around the lake sometimes receives more than 500 inches (1,270 cm) of snow. Each year, the melting snow and spring rains replenish the lake's water supply.

There are no large cities in the Cascades, but there are many communities that were built around the logging mills in the region. The Cascades provide much of Oregon's lumber.

The Eastern High Desert

More than half of Oregon lies on the eastern side of the Cascade Mountains. Large ranches and farms stretch over this region, where cattle are raised and most of the state's wheat is grown. This is an area of few towns, but plenty of wide-open spaces.

Quick Facts

LET IT SNOW
In 1950, Crater Lake National Park received the largest amount of snow that any area of Oregon is ever known to have experienced in a single year. More than 900 inches (2,300 cm) of snow fell on the area.

Visitors from all over the world come to hike and bike at Hells Canyon, the deepest river gorge in the United States.

The Blue Mountains are located near the eastern border of this region. During the gold rush of the 1860s, many people came to this part of Oregon in search of gold. Some of the towns, such as John Day and Baker City, were established by gold miners and business owners who provided goods and services that the miners needed.

Also found in the northeastern corner of the state, along the border with Idaho, is Hells Canyon, the deepest river gorge in the United States. From the highest point on the eastern rim, the canyon is about 8,000 feet (2,400 m) deep, which is even deeper than the Grand Canyon. The Snake River flows through Hells Canyon. The Wallowa Mountains are also found in this region.

The Climate

Because of Oregon's variety of land formations, the weather can be very different from one region to another. People who live along the western coast often experience cool summers and mild winters. Storms drop a great deal of rain on the Coast Range mountains.

The Willamette Valley also receives a steady supply of rain from fall until spring, but the summers are usually dry and hot. Only an occasional winter storm passes over the valley. These storms rarely drop more than a couple of inches of snow. Most of the snow that falls in Oregon lands in the Cascade Mountains, where skiing is a popular sport. Many of the tallest mountains in the

Cascades receive hundreds of inches of snow each year. Eastern Oregon receives the least rainfall, and the people who live in this region experience some of the hottest and some of the coldest temperatures that Oregon offers.

Rainfall and Bodies of Water

People who live outside Oregon often believe that the whole state gets a large amount of rain. However, there are cities in Oregon that do not receive as much rain as some places on the East Coast. For example, New York City receives close to 50 inches (130 cm) of precipitation a year, while Portland receives only about 35 inches (90 cm). There are places in Oregon that get much more rain, however. Laurel Mountain, one of Oregon's wettest places, receives more than 115 inches (290 cm) of precipitation each year. In 1996, Laurel Mountain recorded a state record-breaking 204 inches (518 cm) of rain.

Some of Oregon's rain and snow lands in its rivers and streams. The water from these sources provides drinking water for people and animals, and the rivers also supply electricity (through a series of dams), a means of transportation, and recreational fun. The main rivers of Oregon include the Columbia River, which defines most of the northern boundary between Oregon and Washington, and the Snake River, which makes up much of the eastern boundary between Oregon and Idaho. The Willamette River runs for more than 300 miles (480 km) between Eugene and Portland. Other major rivers include the John Day River in northeastern Oregon, the Rogue River in the southwestern part of the state, and the Klamath River, which lies in the southeastern portion of the state.

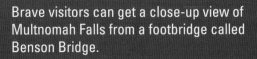

Brave visitors can get a close-up view of Multnomah Falls from a footbridge called Benson Bridge.

The Columbia River cuts across the Cascades through the Columbia River Gorge. This canyon, up to 4,000 feet (1,200 m) deep, is 80 miles (130 km) long and known for its scenic beauty. The highest waterfall in Oregon is Multnomah Falls, located east of Portland on the south side of the Columbia River Gorge. At 620 feet (190 m), Multnomah Falls is among the tallest waterfalls in the United States.

The deep snow in the mountains feeds the many lakes found in Oregon. Crater Lake is the deepest lake in the entire United States, and Wallowa Lake in eastern Oregon is famous for its clear water. Some lakes in southeastern Oregon are surprisingly salty and completely dry up in the summer months. These lakes are usually landlocked, and the water that forms them contains salt or minerals that remain when the water evaporates.

The Pacific Ocean, which hugs Oregon's entire western boundary, is also one of the state's most important bodies of water. Although the waters of the ocean are often too cold for swimming, Oregonians love to walk along the shore, get their feet wet in the waves, and hunt for shells along the beach.

Plants and Wildlife

Nearly half of Oregon is covered in thick forests of cedar, fir, pine, and spruce trees. Before settlers from the eastern United States came to Oregon in large numbers, the land was filled with thick ancient forests, with some of the trees reaching heights of several hundred feet. Only about 10 percent of old-growth forests—which are forests that contain stands of very old trees in which logging has never taken place—remain today. Some of the best places to see these old-growth forests are at Oregon Caves National Monument, outside Cave Junction in southern Oregon; at Union Creek, not far from Crater Lake; in the Three Sisters Wilderness area (part of Willamette National Forest) in central Oregon; and at Lost Lake in Mount Hood National Forest.

In addition to trees, Oregon has many types of wild berries. Blackberry bushes are so numerous and grow so quickly that some people consider them pests, because they are so hard to get rid of. Salmonberry, huckleberry, marionberry, and thimbleberry are other types of edible berries that grow wild in Oregon.

There are many different kinds of ferns that grow well in the wet ground in parts of Oregon. Wood fern and maidenhair are two of these ferns. The horsetail fern—which is not technically a fern—also grows in Oregon's moist soils. It springs up from the ground looking a little like asparagus, but the plant eventually opens its needlelike spines along its top, giving it the appearance of a horse's tail. The damp

Oregon's logging industry has threatened its old-growth forests. Some of these forests can still be seen at Oregon Caves National Monument.

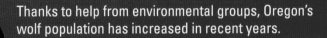
Thanks to help from environmental groups, Oregon's wolf population has increased in recent years.

forests also provide a fertile environment for mosses, lichen, and mushrooms.

Among Oregon's many native animals is a small, mouse-like creature called the vole. Voles are one of the favorite foods of the northern spotted owl, which is a threatened species in Oregon. (A threatened species is at risk, if its numbers continue to decline, of becoming endangered; an endangered species has such low numbers that it is at risk of becoming extinct, or completely dying out.) Because the northern spotted owl is threatened, logging companies are not allowed to cut down trees in the forests where the owls nest. Another forest creature is the northern flying squirrel, which is able to glide from branch to branch. It likes to eat lichen, nuts, and plants.

Bigger animals, such as elk and black-tailed deer, also live in the woods. Higher elevations in the Cascades are home to bighorn sheep and mountain goats, as well as bobcats, wolves, coyotes, foxes, and minks.

Perhaps one of Oregon's best-known creatures is the slug. Different types of slugs can be found throughout the United States, but certain kinds are very common in Oregon. The banana slug is one type that can be found in Oregon's damp soils. It is usually yellow and very slimy. Some banana slugs can grow to be more than 6 inches (15 cm) long. Slugs like to eat plants and flowers, which can be a problem for Oregon's gardeners.

The list of birds that make their homes in Oregon is very long. It includes blackbirds, bluebirds, ducks, geese, eagles, egrets, finches, flickers, nutcrackers, and owls. Oregon is located on the migratory trails of many different kinds of birds. This means that the birds pass through Oregon as they travel during the different seasons. Oregonians may hear different bird songs throughout the year as migrating birds come and go.

Some fish in the region are also migratory. Large numbers of salmon can be found in many of the state's waterways in late summer and fall. Oregon's waters are also home to several different types of trout. Because of overfishing, pollution, and other forms of human interference, wild populations of many types of fish are decreasing. In order to keep the rivers and lakes supplied, many fish farms have been established throughout the state. These farms breed and raise fish to be released into the state's waterways.

Endangered Animals in Oregon

Throughout history, many types of animals around the world have become extinct. This is sometimes a natural process, in which a species dies off. However, in recent history, most extinctions have been caused by human interference. Settlement and pollution have destroyed animal habitats. The overhunting of certain animals has also caused some animal populations to decrease. When an animal population gets dangerously low, the U.S. government or a state government may label the species as "endangered." Federal and state laws attempt to protect endangered species, to try and keep them from becoming extinct.

Endangered animals in Oregon include the gray wolf, the Columbian white-tailed deer, the short-tailed albatross, different types of sea turtles, and the Fender's blue butterfly. Certain types of salmon in the Columbia and Snake rivers are among the state's endangered fish. Threatened species—those that are almost endangered—include the Canada lynx, the northern spotted owl, and the Oregon silver-spot butterfly.

Quick Facts

PROTECTING SALMON

In 1997, the Oregon state government established the Oregon Plan for Salmon and Watersheds. Citizens, local groups, and the state and federal governments now work together to restore the state's salmon population. These groups also work to improve water quality and make watersheds (the land around a river) healthier.

Plants & Animals

Northern Spotted Owl

The northern spotted owl is on Oregon's threatened species list. It is also threatened in the states of Washington and California. The owl is threatened because its habitat—old-growth forests—is quickly disappearing as the large trees in these forests are being cut down.

Skunks

Two species of skunks live in Oregon: the spotted skunk and the striped skunk. Striped skunks, easily recognized by their black coats and white stripes, are larger and more common. They can cause a mess in people's yards and gardens by digging up lawns and eating plants. They can also burrow under porches and get into garbage cans. Skunks are naturally very shy, but if they feel threatened, they may shoot a smelly liquid from their scent glands. They can hit targets as far as 20 feet (6 m) away with this liquid.

Great Blue Heron

The great blue heron lives along saltwater shorelines and around rivers. In Oregon, these herons are found along the Pacific shore or along the banks of some of Oregon's great rivers, such as the Rogue. The bird's feathers are a bluish-gray. It has a black stripe above each eye and very long legs. The wingspan of the great blue heron can be as large as 6 feet (2 m).

Blackberries

Blackberry bushes grow wild in almost all areas of Oregon. They grow in backyards, on the median strips along major highways, and in the woods. Their brambles and leaves are very thorny, and picking them is messy—blackberries can stain fingers and clothes. Once the bushes become established in a homeowner's yard, they are very hard to get rid of—but they reward people with tasty fruit each August.

Pacific Giant Salamander

The Pacific giant salamander is the largest salamander found in Oregon. It also lives in California and Washington. The salamander has a big head and muscular legs and can grow to be 13 inches (33 cm) long. It has a marbled pattern on its skin that is tan and reddish-brown. Salamanders like cool, moist forests and tend to live underground except when they come out at night. The Pacific giant salamander is one of the only salamanders that can make a noise—a sort of low-pitched yelp or bark.

Chinook Salmon

Chinook salmon (sometimes called king salmon) are the largest salmon found in the Pacific Northwest. They are born in freshwater streams. Once they mature, they swim into the ocean. Some salmon travel 2,000 miles (3,200 km) away from their birthplace. After spending several years in the ocean, salmon return to mate in the same stream in which they were hatched. The Chinook salmon is Oregon's state fish.

From the Beginning

Oregon has a long and interesting history. For many years, the region was home to native people who depended on its rich resources. These same riches attracted white settlers in more modern times.

From about 11,500 BCE until the middle of the sixteenth century, the only people who lived in what is now called Oregon were the ancestors of present-day American Indians. Their ancestors, in turn, probably came to North America from Asia, crossing a land bridge that used to connect eastern Russia and Alaska.

The groups that chose present-day Oregon as their new home soon discovered the many different kinds of food that were available. The bays, rivers, and ocean were filled with salmon, shellfish, and sea mammals. The fertile soil in the Willamette Valley and the Rogue River Valley provided wild fruits, nuts, and nutritious roots. The people also benefited from the forests in their new land. The trees supplied wood for homes, tools, and boats. Some of these early people hunted the animals that lived in the woods, such as deer, elk, sheep, and antelope. The groups that settled in the eastern section of present-day Oregon hunted, fished, and gathered seeds for food, and they found enough wood in this grassland region to provide bark and timber to build their homes and boats.

Several different native groups lived throughout the region. The Klamath and the Modoc lived in the south-central part of present-day Oregon. They lived in teepees during the summer and in earthen shelters during the winter. The Paiute,

A replica of Fort Clatsop, where the explorers Lewis and Clark lived in the winter of 1805–1806, can be seen in Astoria.

The Columbia River was an important source of food for many American Indian groups.

who hunted and fished, lived in caves during the harsh winters in the deserts of what is now southeastern Oregon. In the northeastern corner of the region, the Nez Perce, one of the largest groups to live on the Columbia Plateau, used tents for homes. After the Spanish brought horses to North America, the Nez Perce became known for their skills in raising and riding horses. The Cayuse, who lived in the north, were also skilled with horses.

The Clackamas and Kalapuya lived in the Willamette Valley. Along the Pacific Coast were the Clatsop, the Tillamook, the Siuslaw, the Umpqua, and the Coquille. Many of today's Oregonians are familiar with these names because they are used to identify certain rivers and forests in the state.

The First Europeans

It was not until the middle of the sixteenth century that Europeans reached the land that would one day be called Oregon. Some of the first Europeans to come close to these shores were Spanish explorers who were looking for gold. They had heard rumors about secret cities filled with gold in North America. They sailed their ships northward from Mexico, looking for a river that would allow them to sail deeper into the North American continent. But when their ships reached the area around present-day Oregon, heavy storms kept them from getting any closer than the Pacific shoreline. Some people believe that the English explorer Sir Francis Drake reached the southern coast of what is now Oregon in 1579. There is little evidence to support this, however.

Once the rumors of gold spread, many European countries became interested in the Pacific Northwest. Over the years, different countries sent ships up and down the shore, looking for rivers that would allow them to travel across North America. Settlers from Russia and Britain set up fur-trading posts in what is now Alaska and western Canada. Spanish settlers built outposts in the region that includes California. Each of these countries, at one time or another, claimed the land of the Pacific Northwest. In 1775, the Spanish explorer Bruno de Hezeta (sometimes spelled Heceta) may have been the first European to find the mouth of the Columbia River. The currents were too strong for his crew to explore it, however. He thought the body of water was a bay, and he called it Ensenada de Asunción—"Assumption Cove." He claimed the entire surrounding region for Spain. Three years later, the British explorer Captain James Cook landed on Oregon's central coast. He called the area Cape Foulweather.

In 1792, a U.S. captain named Robert Gray successfully guided his ship into the same wild and dangerous river that Hezeta had found. He was the first white

The Columbia River was named after Robert Gray's ship, the *Columbia Rediviva*.

explorer to actually enter the river. Gray named it after his ship, the *Columbia Rediviva*. Other American explorers soon followed, and their discoveries helped support the United States' claim to the land that would become known as the Oregon Country.

The Lewis and Clark Expedition

In 1803, under President Thomas Jefferson's leadership, the United States bought a large area of land called the Louisiana Territory from France. This deal—called the Louisiana Purchase—gave the United States land that extended, east to west, from the Mississippi River to the Rocky Mountains. It included all or part of fourteen current U.S. states. With this land, the country doubled in size. But Jefferson wanted the United States to extend from the Atlantic to the Pacific oceans. He also wanted to find a water route from the eastern United States to the Pacific. To make part of that dream come true, he organized a group of explorers called the Corps of Discovery. Jefferson wanted this group to explore and learn about as much land as possible in western North America, to make maps of the area, and to befriend the native people. The Corps would travel by boat up the Missouri River to its farthest point west and search for a water route that would continue to the Pacific Ocean. Jefferson appointed former army captain Meriwether Lewis to lead the group. Lewis

A statue in Seaside honors the Lewis and Clark Expedition.

asked another former officer, William Clark, to be the co-leader of what became known as the Lewis and Clark Expedition.

Lewis and Clark began their trip in 1804. By the late summer of 1805, they had traveled as far as they could up the Missouri River and reached the western boundary of the Louisiana Territory. They did not find a water route from there to the Pacific—no such route existed. Instead they had to travel over land across the Rocky Mountains. Continuing west, they eventually journeyed by boat down the Snake and Columbia rivers, and by November 1805, they reached the Pacific.

In Their Own Words

We arrived at the great Columbia river, which comes in from the northwest.... The country all round is level, rich and beautiful....

—Patrick Gass, a member of the Lewis and Clark Expedition

They built a camp, called Fort Clatsop, at the mouth of the Columbia River and spent the winter there. Lewis and Clark's trip proved to be a difficult but very important journey. As a result of their exploration, a path was forged that many settlers would soon follow. Although Lewis and Clark did not find the water route they were looking for, reports about their adventures—and about the natural resources of the region they had explored—inspired thousands of other people to move west.

Mountain Men, Fur Trappers, and Missionaries

Fur traders and fur trappers—sometimes referred to as mountain men—came to present-day Oregon from all over the United States and from Canada (controlled by Great Britain in the early 1800s). They were eager to hunt beavers or trade with the Indians for beaver pelts, which could be sold for high prices in eastern North America and in Europe. In 1811, a permanent settlement was built at the mouth of the Columbia River by American businessman John Jacob Astor. This settlement soon became the small town of Astoria.

MISSIONARIES MISLED

It is possible that missionaries came to Oregon as a result of incorrect information. In 1832, a newspaper article reported that four members of the Nez Perce tribe had traveled to St. Louis, Missouri. They may have been looking for William Clark, who was working as the superintendent of Indian affairs in the Louisiana Territory. They may have been in search of better tools and weapons, which they had seen used by members of the Lewis and Clark Expedition. The press reported, however, that they were looking for a new religion and wanted to become Christians. Once missionaries heard this, many of them made plans to travel west.

The missionaries came next. Missionaries traveled west hoping to convert the Indians to Christianity. The first group was led by a minister named Jason Lee. He set up a permanent settlement in the Willamette Valley, near present-day Salem, in 1834. The most famous of the missionaries, however, were Marcus and Narcissa Whitman. The Whitmans did more than preach Christian beliefs to American Indians. They also helped many travelers make the trip to Oregon along a route that became known as the Oregon Trail.

The Oregon Trail

By the 1840s, many people were pouring into the Oregon Country through the Oregon Trail. Thousands of wagon trains made the difficult journey, which for many of the pioneers began in Independence, Missouri, and ended just south of Portland in the small town of Oregon City. (Part of the

In Their Own Words

We were nearing the Cascade Mountains. The oxen were worn out, and the wagons were in poor condition to cross the mountains. . . . Our provisions were exhausted by this time, and for three days we had only salal berries and some soup made by thickening water, from flour shaken from a remaining flour sack."

—Harriet Scott Palmer, who traveled the Oregon Trail as an eleven-year-old in 1852

trail followed the same route that had been taken by Lewis and Clark.) The trip was more than 2,000 miles (3,200 km) long and often took four to five months to complete. The trail crossed three mountain ranges: the Rocky Mountains, the Blue Mountains, and the Cascades. Most people traveled in large covered wagons, called prairie schooners, which were usually pulled by a team of oxen.

Many people died during the journey, but this did not stop the wagon trains. People from the eastern United States (and elsewhere) had caught "Oregon Fever," and they were eager to find what they hoped would be a new and wonderful life once they reached the Willamette Valley.

The Oregon Trail Interpretive Center near Baker City features exhibits about life on the Oregon Trail.

MAKING A PINWHEEL

Children on wagon trains going to Oregon often made their own games and toys. One simple toy was the pinwheel. Many boys and girls made pinwheels and attached them to the wagons—the colors would spin as the wagon moved or as the wind blew.

WHAT YOU NEED

1 sheet of heavy paper (a file folder, oak tag, or thick construction paper)

Ruler	Sharpened pencil
Scissors	Crayons or markers
1 straight pin	Long unsharpened pencil with an eraser

Use the ruler and pencil to draw a 6-inch (15 cm) square on the paper. Cut out the square with the scissors. Using the ruler, draw diagonal lines from each corner, but stop each line 1 inch (2.5 cm) from the center of the square.

Draw a dot in the center of the square.

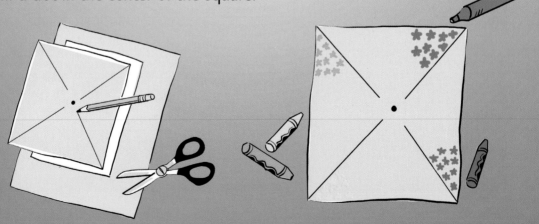

Using the crayons or markers, draw small circles or stars in part of each of the corners. (Color only the corners shown in the illustration.)

Use the scissors to cut along the diagonal lines you drew earlier. Make sure you stop cutting about 1 inch (2.5 cm) from the center.

With the decorated side of the paper facing away from you, bend each decorated corner toward you so that all four points meet at the center. Overlap the tips a little bit.

Place the unsharpened pencil behind the paper, with the eraser against the center. Push the pin through the four tips, then through the center. The sharp end of the pin should stick into the pencil's eraser. Be careful not to stick your finger when you push the pin through the paper.

Blow on the pinwheel or put it outside in the wind, and watch the colors spin. You can experiment with different colors and designs to see what neat patterns the spinning colors make.

The Road to Statehood

In the early 1800s both the United States and Great Britain claimed the Oregon Country, a region largely made up of what is now the U.S. states of Oregon, Washington, and Idaho and most of the Canadian province of British Columbia. Under an 1818 treaty, the United States and Britain agreed to share the region. But as more and more Americans traveled the Oregon Trail and settled in the Oregon Country, the U.S. government claimed that the United States should have sole control of the area. In 1846, the two nations reached a compromise. Britain gave up its claim to land south of the 49th parallel (49 degrees north latitude), which is now the northern border of the state of Washington. The United States gave up its claim to land north of the parallel.

With the dispute over control of the region resolved, many settlers in what is now Oregon wanted their new homeland to become a U.S. state. As a step in that direction, in 1848, Congress passed a measure, which was signed by President James K. Polk, establishing the Oregon Territory. The territory originally included the land that would eventually become the states of Oregon, Washington, and Idaho, as well as parts of Montana and Wyoming.

Two years later, Congress passed the Oregon Donation Land Act. This law gave more than 300 acres (120 hectares) of free land to anyone who promised to plant crops on it. The idea of free land brought a new wave of people to Oregon. In 1851, gold was discovered in southern and eastern Oregon. By the 1860s, Oregon—like California before it—experienced a gold rush.

With all these trappers, missionaries, settlers, and gold miners rushing into Oregon, the American Indian population began to suffer. In 1805, it was estimated that more than 40,000 Indians lived in the region. Their numbers were decreasing, however. The trappers and other new residents were hunting and killing animals that the Indians had once relied on for food. The settlers were claiming land that had belonged to the Indians. The miners polluted the waters when they dug for gold, killing fish and making the water unsafe to drink.

White people also brought with them diseases, such as measles, to which the Indians had never been exposed and had no natural immunity. In 1847, measles broke out at Marcus and Narcissa Whitman's mission school in Waiilatpu (located just north of the present Oregon-Washington border). Many Cayuse children died, and Cayuse warriors blamed the Whitmans. The warriors attacked the mission buildings, killing the Whitmans and twelve other whites. A group of white militia responded by attacking a group of Cayuse who had not been involved in the first attack. The conflict escalated into the Cayuse War, which lasted until 1850. There were also tensions between settlers and other tribes. More wars followed, including the Rogue River War of 1855–1856. The Indians were not able to drive out the white settlers, but they still fought to try to protect and reclaim their land. Federal troops

Narcissa Whitman began a mission school with her husband, Marcus. They were killed when the school was burned down in 1847.

This picture shows Chief Joseph surrendering in 1877.

became involved, and many Indians were moved to reservations as their land was taken over by whites.

In the middle of all this, in 1857, a convention was called to write a state constitution for Oregon. (By this time, the original Oregon Territory had been divided in two: a smaller Oregon Territory and a separate Washington Territory.) Two years later, on February 14, 1859, Oregon (with its present boundaries) became the thirty-third state.

Conflicts between white settlers and Indians persisted after statehood, and wars continued to break out over the next twenty years. In 1877, the U.S. Army ordered Chief Joseph—leader of the Nez Perce—to take his people from their traditional home in eastern Oregon to a reservation in present-day Idaho. After Nez Perce warriors retaliated by raiding a settlement and killing several whites, Chief Joseph tried to lead his people to Canada. Army troops followed them, with battles fought along the way. In the end, Chief Joseph surrendered after many of his people had frozen or starved to death. Joseph and his people were sent to a reservation in present-day Oklahoma, where many of them died from disease. Oregon's overall Indian population continued to decrease in size. By the end of the 1800s, fewer than 10,000 American Indians remained in the state.

In Their Own Words

Hear me, my chiefs. I am tired. My heart is sick and sad. From where the sun now stands I will fight no more forever.

—Chief Joseph, upon his surrender to the U.S. Army

Modern Times and Growing Pains

When a transcontinental railroad line reached Oregon in the 1880s— enabling people to go from the eastern United States to Oregon by train—travel to the new state became much easier, and the number of people living in Oregon grew rapidly. Between 1900 and 1910, for instance, Portland's population grew from about 90,000 to more than 200,000. Some of the people who arrived in Oregon during this time were not as interested in being farmers or ranchers as the settlers who had come before them. Many of these new residents were used to living in cities, so they developed Oregon's cities instead, building new stores and other types of businesses.

A transcontinental railroad line reached Oregon in the 1880s, causing the state's population to grow.

The railroad also provided a way of transporting goods from Oregon to other parts of the nation. Wheat and lumber grown in Oregon could now be shipped east. This meant that more people could buy these products, and Oregon's economy began to grow. Factories were built in Oregon's cities, creating jobs for many residents.

Around the turn of the twentieth century, people other than those of European descent began to move to Oregon. Many immigrants from Asia—particularly from Japan and China—made Oregon their home. By 1900, Portland had the second-largest "Chinatown" in the United States (after San Francisco, California). The African-American community also increased in population during this time.

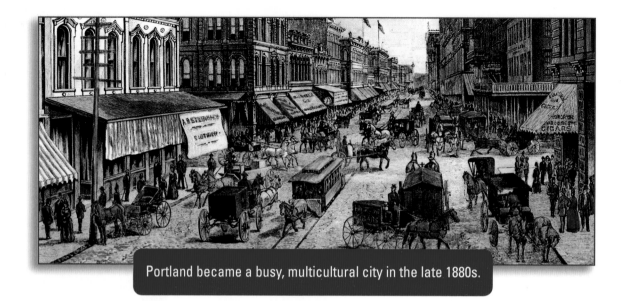

Portland became a busy, multicultural city in the late 1880s.

Despite the fact that the early settlers of Oregon were often intolerant of people who were not white, a racially mixed population in Oregon continued to expand.

Hard times hit Oregon—and the rest of the nation—with the Great Depression. Starting in 1929, this was a period of time when the country's economy was in terrible shape. Banks and businesses closed, and many people lost their jobs and their homes. The federal government established programs to help the unemployed find work while also rebuilding the country. Workers were hired for such projects as constructing roads, logging forests, and building dams. Many Oregonians helped build the Bonneville Dam, which was completed in 1938. By taming the current of the Columbia River, the dam helped create electric power for homes and businesses throughout the Pacific Northwest. The reservoir behind the dam provided irrigation water for farms. The availability of inexpensive electricity also helped to make Portland one of the nation's major shipbuilding centers.

World War II began in Europe in 1939, with the United States joining the war in December 1941, after Japan attacked the U.S. naval base at Pearl Harbor, Hawaii. The

Quick Facts

JAPANESE SHELLING
In June 1942, a Japanese submarine fired shells on Fort Stevens, at the mouth of the Columbia River on the Oregon side. It was the only time during World War II that there was hostile shelling of a military base on the U.S. mainland.

In Their Own Words

At Bonneville now there are ships in the locks, The waters have risen and cleared all the rocks, Shiploads of plenty will steam past the docks, So roll on, Columbia, roll on.

—Lyrics from folksinger Woody Guthrie's 1941 song "Roll On, Columbia"

war helped improve the U.S. economy. Factories needed workers to make supplies for the war effort. Oregon's urban areas became important manufacturing centers for war materials, and the state's farms helped supply the troops with food.

After World War II ended, Oregon entered a period of relative prosperity. There was increased demand for the state's lumber and beef, and electricity was brought to remote areas. As a result of the tapping of new water sources, land that had once been dry could now be planted. New highway construction helped bring tourists to see the state's wonders. There were challenges, however, for some people. Small farmers faced increased competition from larger farms whose owners could afford new machinery and chemicals for their crops. The overall rural farm population dropped, causing hardships for small towns.

It was also during the 1950s and 1960s that Oregonians began to notice that some of their industries were causing great environmental damage. Factories had turned the Willamette River into a sewer, contaminating the water with their waste. In other places, entire mountainsides had been stripped of trees by the

lumber industry. This caused dangerous mudslides that clogged rivers and damaged homes. Oregonians became determined to make their state healthy again.

In the 1950s and 1960s, Oregon enacted a number of laws to protect and clean up the environment. By the 1970s, Oregon became the state with the most laws that had been created to protect natural resources.

Oregon Today

Oregon is a state that is rich in natural beauty. Its wide range of natural resources, however, needs to be taken care of. Today, the people of Oregon know that they cannot overfish their rivers or the fish will become endangered. They know that if too many forests are cleared by the logging industry, this logging will destroy plant and animal habitats and cause mudslides. Oregonians are committed to keeping their state healthy and clean. This not only makes Oregon a great place to live—it also attracts people from other states who enjoy visiting Oregon's beaches, mountains, and deserts. The money that tourists spend helps to create jobs.

Although Oregon is changing, in many ways it also remains the same. Just as in the pioneer days, people from all over the nation still hear that Oregon is a great place to live. In fact, it is among the fastest growing states in the nation, with its diverse population increasing 12 percent between 2000 and 2010. The air quality is good. The temperatures are mild. And the natural environment offers many exciting outdoor adventures. Traveling to Oregon is far easier than it used to be hundreds of years ago, and when people come to the state, they still find a land of green rolling hills and a great place to establish a new home.

Important Dates

★ **11,500** BCE The first native peoples make their homes in what is now Oregon.

★ **1543** Spanish navigator Bartolomé Ferrelo becomes the first European explorer to sight the Oregon coast.

★ **1775** Bruno de Hezeta is possibly the first European to find the mouth of the Columbia River and claims the land around it for Spain.

★ **1778** British explorer Captain James Cook lands on Oregon's central coast.

★ **1792** American Robert Gray successfully guides his ship, the *Columbia Rediviva*, into the river that he will later name in honor of his ship. He claims the Oregon Country for the United States.

★ **1843** Pioneers in large numbers begin a major migration to the Oregon Country along the Oregon Trail.

★ **1844** Slavery is declared illegal in the Oregon Country by the region's Provisional Government.

★ **1845** Francis Pettygrove names the new city on the Columbia River after his hometown of Portland, Maine.

★ **1848** The U.S. Congress establishes the Oregon Territory.

★ **1851** Gold is discovered in southern and eastern Oregon.

★ **1859** On February 14, Oregon becomes the thirty-third state.

★ **1877** The U.S. Army orders Chief Joseph of the Nez Perce to take his people from their home in Oregon to a reservation in present-day Idaho.

★ **1883** A transcontinental railroad reaches Portland.

★ **1938** The Bonneville Dam on the Columbia River is completed, providing electrical power for homes and businesses and irrigation water for farms.

★ **1951** Oregon passes the country's first laws to combat air pollution.

★ **1990** Oregonians elect their first female governor, Barbara Roberts.

★ **2010** In the middle of tough economic times, voters in Oregon approve two measures increasing the taxes paid by people with high incomes, to help pay for education and social services.

The People

The people who have lived in Oregon—from the earliest inhabitants thousands of years ago to the people currently living in the state—have shown an independent spirit and an appreciation for the riches of their land.

Early People

Very little is known about the earliest people who lived on the land that is now Oregon. Many historians assume, however, that the rich food sources found along the Pacific Coast helped to feed Oregon's first inhabitants. They probably existed on a diet that included clams, salmon, oysters, seals, and whales. Many of these early people probably traveled by water—up and down the ocean coast as well as into the interior of the land, using the many rivers and creeks. The fertile valleys of the Willamette and Rogue rivers provided fruits and nuts.

The beliefs of the many different groups varied, but people who have studied their history think that the original residents of the region were very aware of protecting the environment. They lived in the area for many thousands of years with little sign of pollution or of endangering the wildlife. "Over time," writes Gordon B. Dodds in his book *The American Northwest*, "the first inhabitants worked out a system of land management that enabled them both to use and to conserve natural resources."

A mother and daughter celebrate Oregon's heritage in traditional pioneer dresses.

The Klamath lived in southern Oregon and fished from Klamath Lake.

A little more is known about some of the later people who lived in the area. One of those groups was the Klamath, who lived in the southernmost part of the area. They moved according to the season. In the winter, they lived inside dwellings they built. In other seasons, they lived largely in the open, sleeping in teepees, and followed the trails of animals, which provided them with food. The men hunted animals such as deer, antelope, and sheep. They used spears and nets to catch fish and ate the eggs of swans, ducks, and other birds that lived on Klamath Lake.

Another group was the Paiute, who lived on the easternmost part of what is now Oregon, a harsh land that is dry and very hot in the summer and very cold in the winter. The Paiute tended to live in caves because they were continually moving in search of food. Their main sources of food were rabbit and antelope.

The Chinook lived along the rivers and the ocean shoreline. They were one of the largest American Indian groups and some of the most

MISTAKEN IDENTITY

The Nez Perce, who lived in northeastern Oregon, called themselves Nee-Me-Poo (or Nimiipu), which means "real people." They were given the name Nez Perce, which means "pierced noses," by French traders, but the Nez Perce did not pierce their noses. The French apparently confused them with another Indian group that did this.

successful traders. The Chinook's ability to trade made them one of the richest Indian groups in all of North America. They also developed a special language that helped them speak to European traders, whether the traders came from French- or English-speaking countries. This language was called Chinook Jargon and was made up of French, English, and Indian words.

Other American Indian groups included the Clatsop, Clackamas, Puyallup, Nisqually, Tillamook, Siuslaw, and Umpqua. Many of these groups were completely wiped out by diseases brought

The Umatilla Indian Reservation is in the northeastern part of the state. The reservation is home to about 2,700 people.

to the region by Europeans or by Americans of European descent.

Today, Oregon is home to several Indian reservations. They include the Confederated Tribes of the Umatilla Indian Reservation in northeastern Oregon, which includes members of the Cayuse, the Umatilla, and the Walla Walla. The Confederated Tribes of Warm Springs Reservation is located on the eastern slopes of the Cascades. This is where the Warm Springs tribe, the Wasco, and the Paiute live. On the Pacific Coast is the Confederated Tribes of Grand Ronde Reservation, which has the largest population of all the reservations in Oregon. A reservation for the Klamath Tribes—the Klamath, the Modoc, and the Yahooskin—is planned for an area of south-central Oregon.

Most of Oregon's American Indians do not live on reservations, however. There were about 64,000 Indians living in the state in 2008. Of this number, approximately 90 percent did not live on reservations.

In recent years, American Indian groups have appealed to the U.S. government to abide by treaties that have been ignored for a long time. These treaties were supposed to grant certain rights and property to American Indian groups. In the past, in an attempt to bring the Indian population into the main culture of the United States, government recognition of many Indian groups was officially "terminated." This meant the end of federal support for tribal sovereignty, or independence. The government thought this would help the Indians. However, in many cases, it did not, and the federal government recognized the failure of the termination policy. Today, government officials are working to reestablish traditional Indian groups and to make new laws that will protect their rights.

Different Times, Different People

The first explorers to see what is now Oregon were the Spanish, in the 1500s. In the years that followed, other explorers came to the area, including Lewis and Clark in the early 1800s. Fur trappers, missionaries, and those seeking gold were also drawn to the region. Beginning in the 1840s, many thousands of settlers from the eastern United States traveled the Oregon Trail to start new lives in Oregon.

During the late nineteenth and early twentieth centuries, people from all over the world, including Europe and Asia, came to Oregon. Many of these immigrants came to the state with special skills, which helped them find jobs in their new homeland. Many Greek people worked on the railroads, many Swedish people worked in the lumber mills, and many people from Norway and Finland made careers in the fishing industry. People from Denmark and Italy often turned to farming, while those from Ireland and Mexico found jobs using their skills in mining.

Many people from China came to Oregon in the second half of the nineteenth century, often to escape political problems and poverty in their homeland. These immigrants often found jobs in Oregon's mines, in fish-packing industries along the Columbia River, and especially working on the railroads. It was through the hard labor and courage of many Chinese men that Oregon's railroad lines were completed. Chinese immigrants faced a great deal of prejudice and discrimination, however. Many lived in separate areas of towns called Chinatowns.

Quick Facts

SCANDINAVIAN ORIGINS
Junction City, located outside Eugene, was settled by people from Denmark, Finland, Norway, and Sweden. To celebrate their Scandinavian heritage, the people of Junction City transform their downtown into an authentic old-world village every summer when they hold their Scandinavian Festival. They dress in authentic costumes, dance to traditional music, and cook traditional foods.

Famous Oregonians

Chief Joseph: Native American Leader

Chief Joseph was born in what is now northeastern Oregon, around 1840. He became chief of the Nez Perce at a time when white settlers were moving to the area and demanding that the Nez Perce give up their land. At first, the government allowed the Nez Perce to stay on their land, but later this ruling was changed. After bloodshed broke out between white settlers and the Nez Perce, Chief Joseph tried to lead his people to safety in Canada. In the end, however, he and his people were captured, taken to what is now Oklahoma, and eventually relocated on a small reservation in Washington State. He died in 1904.

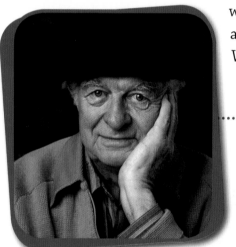

Linus Pauling: Scientist

Linus Pauling was born in Portland in 1901. He received his bachelor's degree from Oregon State College, where he studied chemistry. He also received a doctorate from the California Institute of Technology. Pauling taught and did research for many years. He was awarded the Presidential Medal of Merit in 1948 for his research work during World War II and the Nobel Prize in Chemistry in 1954. Later in life, he became an anti-war activist and was awarded the Nobel Peace Prize in 1962. He is one of only two people awarded two Nobel Prizes in different fields. (Marie Curie is the other.) Pauling died in 1994.

Beverly Cleary: Author

Born in McMinnville in 1916, Beverly Cleary grew up on a farm in Yamhill and in Portland. She is the writer of many well-known, award-winning children's books. Her most famous character is Ramona Quimby, who is honored in Portland's Beverly Cleary Sculpture Garden. In 2010, some of Cleary's characters were brought to life in the movie *Ramona and Beezus*, starring Selena Gomez as Ramona's big sister Beezus.

Phil Knight: Business Leader

Phil Knight was born in 1938 in Portland. He graduated from the University of Oregon, where he ran track. In 1964, he and his former track coach, Bill Bowerman, started an athletic footwear distribution company. The company would eventually become Nike, one of the leading sportswear and athletic supply businesses in the world. Knight became a billionaire. He and his wife have donated millions of dollars to his Portland high school and to various colleges and medical centers in Oregon. He is a member of the Oregon Sports Hall of Fame.

Matt Groening: Cartoonist

The creator of the television show *The Simpsons*, Matt Groening was born in Portland in 1954. His father, whose name is Homer, was a cartoonist who encouraged his son to draw. In 1985, Matt Groening created an animated family that was featured in short segments on *The Tracey Ullman Show*. In 1990, the characters became the stars of their own popular series. *The Simpsons* surpassed *Gunsmoke* in 2009 to become television's longest-running primetime show.

Ann Curry: Journalist

Ann Curry was born in 1956 in Guam, where her father was stationed with the U.S. Navy. She was raised in Ashland and graduated with a degree in journalism from the University of Oregon in 1978. She began her career as a television reporter at a Medford station and later went to work at a station in Portland. She has won numerous prizes for her television reporting, including four Emmy Awards. Since 1997, she has worked as the news anchor for NBC's *Today Show*, and she is often also seen on the program *Dateline NBC*.

People of many different ethnic backgrounds make their home in Oregon today.

African Americans and Other Groups

The first African American came to present-day Oregon with Captain Robert Gray in the late 1700s. Marcus Lopius worked on Gray's ship. Tragically, he was killed by a group of Tillamook warriors when he went ashore to survey the land. Another legendary African American was Moses Harris, a fur trapper and mountain man, who later became a guide for people traveling the Oregon Trail. There were not

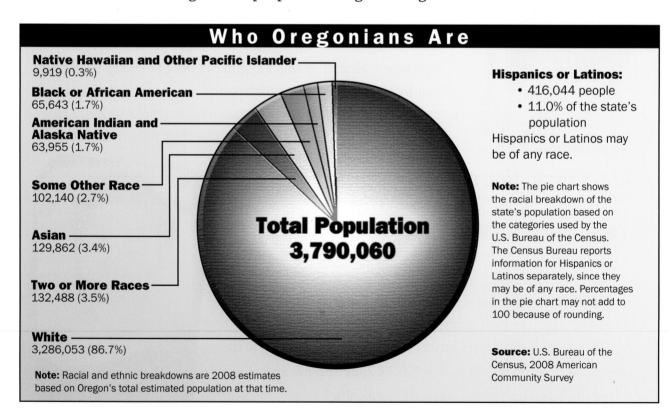

Who Oregonians Are

Native Hawaiian and Other Pacific Islander
9,919 (0.3%)

Black or African American
65,643 (1.7%)

American Indian and Alaska Native
63,955 (1.7%)

Some Other Race
102,140 (2.7%)

Asian
129,862 (3.4%)

Two or More Races
132,488 (3.5%)

White
3,286,053 (86.7%)

Total Population 3,790,060

Hispanics or Latinos:
- 416,044 people
- 11.0% of the state's population

Hispanics or Latinos may be of any race.

Note: The pie chart shows the racial breakdown of the state's population based on the categories used by the U.S. Bureau of the Census. The Census Bureau reports information for Hispanics or Latinos separately, since they may be of any race. Percentages in the pie chart may not add to 100 because of rounding.

Note: Racial and ethnic breakdowns are 2008 estimates based on Oregon's total estimated population at that time.

Source: U.S. Bureau of the Census, 2008 American Community Survey

many African Americans living in Oregon before it became a state, yet some white settlers were concerned that African Americans and Indians might join forces and start a rebellion. So although Oregonians declared their homeland an anti-slavery state in 1857 when they wrote Oregon's constitution, they also prohibited free African Americans from living in the state. This prohibition remained in the constitution until 1926, when a majority of Oregonians voted to remove it.

Today, people of many different ethnic backgrounds live in Oregon, though the population remains mostly white. According to 2008 figures from the U.S. Census Bureau, 1.7 percent of Oregonians are American Indian, 1.7 percent are African American, and 3.4 percent are Asian American. The Hispanic population is the fastest growing minority group in the state, making up 11 percent of the total population.

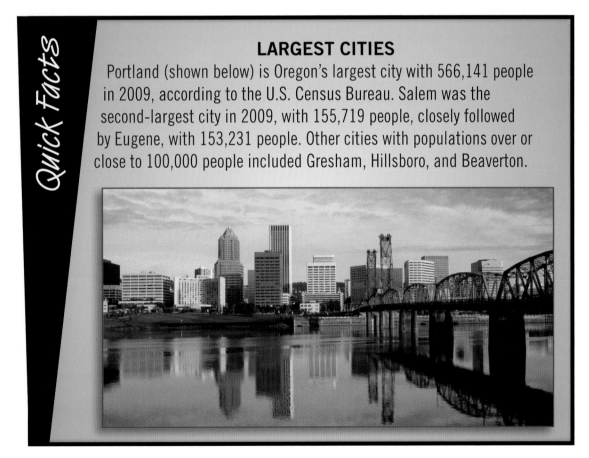

Quick Facts

LARGEST CITIES
Portland (shown below) is Oregon's largest city with 566,141 people in 2009, according to the U.S. Census Bureau. Salem was the second-largest city in 2009, with 155,719 people, closely followed by Eugene, with 153,231 people. Other cities with populations over or close to 100,000 people included Gresham, Hillsboro, and Beaverton.

The Oregon Museum of Science and Industry runs a program for kids called the Cascade Science School. The students shown here are taking notes at Paulina Lake.

Education

More than 550,000 students are enrolled in grades kindergarten through twelve in Oregon's public schools. In 2006, Oregon spent an average of $9,257 per pupil to educate students in these grades. (The national average that year was $10,400 per student.) Oregon has seventeen two-year community colleges and a state university system with seven colleges and universities. These include the University of Oregon in Eugene, Portland State University in Portland, and Oregon State University in Corvallis. The state also has many private colleges and universities. One is Reed College, founded in 1908 in Portland, which is regarded as one of the most challenging colleges in the United States. Willamette University in Salem, which was founded as the Oregon Institute in 1842, is the oldest college in the Pacific Northwest.

Approximately 28 percent of Oregonians have a college bachelor's degree, which is about the national average. The state has set a goal of raising that figure to 40 percent by the year 2025.

Oregon's state university system includes the University of Oregon in Eugene. The school was established in 1872.

Calendar of Events

★ Oregon Asian Celebration

In February, Eugene presents its Oregon Asian Celebration at the Lane County Fairgrounds. Two days of festivities include dance performances, food, demonstrations of martial arts, and exhibitions of ink paintings, bonsai, and other Asian arts.

★ Oregon Scottish Heritage Festival

In April, the Oregon Scottish Society presents an all-day celebration at the Linn County Fair & Expo Center in Albany. The festival provides a taste of Scotland with traditional Scottish music, entertainment, and food.

★ Columbia Gorge Fiddle Contest

During the first weekend in May, Hood River sponsors three days of fiddle workshops, concerts, and food. There are also contests for fiddlers of all ages, who are asked to play three different songs perfectly in less than four minutes.

★ Summer Kite Festival

In June, Lincoln City holds its Summer Kite Festival. Children can make their own kites, and everyone can watch all types of kites fly. A kids' parade is held on the beach in the afternoon. Lincoln City also hosts two other kite festivals—the Fall Kite Festival in October and the Indoor Kite Festival in March.

★ Celtic Festival and Scottish Highland Games

This annual event is held each August at the Jefferson County Fairgrounds in Madras. Athletes compete in traditional Scottish Highland games, including the caber toss and hammer throw. Bagpipes, dances, children's games, food, and fun are all available.

★ Homowo Festival of African Arts

This celebration, held in August, is the largest festival of African music, dance, arts, children's activities, and food presented in the Pacific Northwest. The festival, held on the campus of Portland State University, is intended to re-create the harvest celebration of the Ga people of the African country of Ghana.

★ Fiesta Latina

At this festival, held in September in Island Park in Springfield, Oregonians and visitors to the state can celebrate Hispanic culture with music and fun. Visitors can join the dancing, enjoy the food, and learn about the arts and crafts of Latin America during this weekend party.

★ Pendleton Round-Up

This annual four-day event, held in September, first took place in 1910. It is now one of the ten largest rodeo events in the world. The round-up features all types of rodeo competitions, such as calf roping and steer wrestling. There are also parades, cowboy breakfasts, barbecues, rodeo clowns, and American Indian dances.

★ Greek Festival

Portland's Greek-American community sponsors a three-day festival in October. The festival, held on the grounds of Holy Trinity Greek Orthodox Church, is the perfect place to learn about and enjoy Greek culture, food, and music.

★ Portland's ZooLights

From late November to the beginning of January, visitors can take a ride through the Oregon Zoo on a train decorated with thousands of lights. A variety of musical groups sing traditional and seasonal songs, and there are also holiday treats to eat and animal characters to entertain young visitors.

How the Government Works

I n the early 1800s, there was not one set of laws governing the people of present-day Oregon. Indian groups governed themselves under tribal laws. Canadian fur trappers and traders, as well as other settlers from Canada, which was then controlled by Great Britain, considered themselves governed by British law. However, especially by the 1840s, more and more of the Oregon Country's population consisted of people who had come from, or whose families had come from, the eastern United States. In 1843, a group of 102 American settlers came together and decided to set up a provisional (temporary) government. This group of settlers also selected a committee to write a constitution. The constitution was called the Organic Act, and when it was adopted on July 5, the Provisional Government of Oregon was born.

Quick Facts

CAPITALS

Salem is Oregon's state capital, but other cities have served as the area's capital in the past. When the Oregon Territory was established, Oregon City was named the first territorial capital. Salem became the territorial capital in 1851 and remained so until 1855, when Corvallis held the title for a few months. Later that year, Salem became the capital again—this time to stay.

Oregon's elected officials meet at the State Capitol in Salem.

The Oregon Pioneer statue stands on top of the Capitol Building. The statue is lit by solar-powered floodlights at night.

The Provisional Government had the same basic form as the government of the United States. It had an executive branch, a legislature, and a judicial system. However, there was not a governor heading the executive branch; instead, a committee of three people shared this role. This division of responsibility did not prove to be very successful, though, so in 1845, George Abernethy became the first and only provisional governor of the Oregon Country.

Oregon became a U.S. territory in 1848. Territorial governors were appointed by the president of the United States until Oregon's present-day constitution was adopted

Branches of Government

EXECUTIVE ★ ★ ★ ★ ★ ★ ★ ★

The governor of Oregon serves as the head of the executive branch. The governor is elected to a four-year term and cannot serve more than two terms. He or she is responsible for appointing the heads of many agencies, proposing the state budget, and approving or rejecting proposed laws, among other duties. Other elected positions in the executive branch are the attorney general, the secretary of state, the commissioner of labor and industries, the superintendent of public instruction, and the treasurer.

LEGISLATIVE ★ ★ ★ ★ ★ ★ ★ ★

The legislative branch of government makes the laws. The Oregon legislature, called the legislative assembly, is made up of two houses (or chambers)—the state senate and the state house of representatives. There are thirty senators and sixty representatives. Senators are elected to four-year terms and representatives to two-year terms. There are no limits to the number of terms that legislators can serve.

JUDICIAL ★ ★ ★ ★ ★ ★ ★ ★

The judicial branch is responsible for seeing that the laws are followed and that state laws do not violate the Oregon constitution. The supreme court is the highest court in the state. There are seven supreme court justices. Ten judges serve on the next highest court, the court of appeals. Most trials are held in the circuit courts. There are 173 judges serving on these courts. Circuit court decisions can be appealed to the court of appeals, and sometimes further appealed to the supreme court. All judges, no matter in which court they serve, are elected to a six-year term. There is also a tax court, where judges make decisions on issues involving different types of taxes.

in 1857. Then, "Honest John" Whiteaker was elected governor in 1858, when Oregon was still a territory. He continued as governor after Oregon became a state in 1859.

Oregon's Modern Government

The basic form of Oregon's state government has not changed significantly over the years. The state government has three branches—the executive, legislative,

Portland's elected officials meet at City Hall. The building received a $29 million renovation in the late 1990s.

and judicial branches—which work to make laws and make sure that the laws are obeyed and that they agree with the state constitution.

Oregon also has local governments that serve its cities and counties. Oregon's cities use a form of home rule, which means each city has the right to choose its own form of government. The people of Portland elect a mayor, four commissioners, and an auditor to guide their city. In other cities, a city manager or mayor and a council take care of government affairs. Each of Oregon's thirty-six counties also has its own government. In each county, elected members work together on a board of commissioners.

How a Bill Becomes a Law

All of Oregon's laws begin with an idea. This idea can come from just about anyone: an ordinary citizen, a group of citizens or an organization, a member of the state legislature, or the governor, to name just a few possibilities. A proposed law that is considered in the legislature is called a bill. Bills may create new laws, remove or amend (change) old laws, or provide money for special projects. In order for a bill to become a law, it must go through many different steps. First, the idea (if it does not originate with a member of the legislature) is given to either a state senator or representative, who must sponsor the bill, or accept responsibility for it. If the bill is sponsored by a senator, then it is first worked on in the senate. If it is sponsored by a representative, then it is first worked on in the house of representatives.

The senator or representative sponsoring the bill gives it to lawyers in the Legislative Counsel office, where it is written in correct legal language. Then a special number is assigned to the bill by the chief clerk of the senate or house. Before it returns to the senate or the house, it is printed and read one more time by the lawyers.

The bill is then returned to either the senate or the house for its first official reading. After the senators or representatives have all heard it, the bill is sent to a committee. The members of the committee consider the bill, and the committee may hold hearings to get reactions to the bill from members of the public and from organizations that may be affected by the bill. If the committee votes to pass the bill, it is returned to where it started—either the senate or the house—and read again. Committee members might have changed the bill when they were considering it, so everyone must be brought up to date on those amendments, or changes. The bill is then read for the third time, and this time the members of the

A mural at the front of the state senate chamber depicts the people of Portland hearing the news of Oregon's statehood in 1859.

senate or house vote on it. In order to pass, the bill must receive at least thirty-one votes in the house or sixteen votes in the senate.

A bill that has passed in one chamber then goes to the other chamber, where the whole process of being considered is repeated. Sometimes, the second chamber makes changes to the bill before passing it. Then, a group made up of members from both chambers—called a conference committee—must arrive at a final version of the bill. Both the senate and the house must vote to accept the bill's final version.

After a bill has passed in both the senate and the house in exactly the same form, it is sent to the governor. If the governor signs it, the bill becomes law. The governor

Contacting Lawmakers

★ ★ ★ ★ ★ ★ ★ ★ ★ ★ ★ ★

If you are interested in learning about Oregon's legislators, you can go to this website: **http://www.leg.state.or.us/index.html** There, you will find information about current legislation. If you type in your address and click "submit," you will be told your state and U.S. legislators.

also has the power to veto, or reject, the bill. If this happens, the senate and the house members can vote for it again. If two-thirds of the members of the senate and the house vote in favor of the bill, then they can override the governor's veto, and the bill becomes a law.

Not all state laws have to be passed by the legislature. One of the most interesting things about Oregon's government is what is called the Oregon System. Under the Oregon System, citizens can play a major role in making laws and changing the state constitution—through what is called the initiative process. If citizens who want a new law or a constitutional change gather a specific number of signatures from Oregon voters, their idea—the initiative—will be put to a vote in a general election. This means that everyone in the state can vote on the initiative. If it gets a majority vote, it becomes a state law or constitutional amendment.

Oregon in the Federal Government

Like all states, Oregon is represented in the U.S. Congress in Washington, D.C. Each state has two senators in the U.S. Senate. The number of members each state has in the U.S. House of Representatives is determined by the state's population, with states that have larger populations having more members. California has the most, with 53. Some states have only one. In 2011, Oregon had five representatives.

Making a Living

Oregon's economy has come a long way from the days when fur trapping or trading was the best way to earn a living. Although fur trapping is no longer a business in Oregon, three things that provided early settlers with a good life still bring a great deal of money to the state today. These three things are Oregon's thick forests, its fertile soils, and its abundant seafood.

Forest Products

Since the nineteenth century, Oregon's forests have provided lumber for the entire nation. New houses all over the United States are often built with Oregon lumber. The state is the largest lumber producer in the United States, and it is one of the top suppliers of wood and wood products worldwide. Oregon also leads the nation in the production of Christmas trees, which are grown specifically to be cut down in the winter for the holidays. Oregonians are not the only people who enjoy these trees. Oregon's Christmas trees are shipped throughout the country. Paper and cardboard, made from wood from Oregon's trees, are the products of another big business in the state. The manufacturing of lumber and wood products once provided jobs to many people in Oregon. The number of jobs has dropped significantly, but Oregon's lumber industry is still important to the state. Exports from the state of forest and wood products totaled more than $800 million in 2008.

Fishing is an important part of Oregon's tourism industry.

Workers & Industries

Industry	Number of People Working in That Industry	Percentage of All Workers Who Are Working in That Industry
Education and health care	373,754	20.3%
Wholesale and retail businesses	295,056	16.0%
Manufacturing	226,642	12.3%
Publishing, media, entertainment, hotels, and restaurants	199,135	10.8%
Professionals, scientists, and managers	181,305	9.9%
Construction	140,018	7.6%
Banking and finance, insurance, and real estate	114,455	6.2%
Other services	90,812	4.9%
Transportation and public utilities	82,917	4.5%
Government	77,301	4.2%
Farming, fishing, forestry, and mining	58,895	3.2%
Totals	**1,840,290**	**100%**

Notes: Figures above do not include people in the armed forces. "Professionals" includes people such as doctors and lawyers. Percentages may not add to 100 because of rounding.

Source: U.S. Bureau of the Census, 2008 estimates

Oregon is the largest lumber producer in the nation.

Agriculture

Agriculture is big business in Oregon. In 2007, there were more than 38,000 farms in the state. The average size of a farm was 425 acres (170 ha), and most farms were run by families, not big corporations. Most of Oregon's farms are located in Marion, Clackamas, Morrow, Umatilla, and Washington counties.

Oregon's good climate and fertile soil make the state a wonderful place to grow approximately 250 different products. The major crops that are grown

FROZEN FRIES

One of Oregon's most popular products is frozen French fries. Many of the fries served in fast food restaurants around the country are made from Oregon potatoes.

Quick Facts

include hazelnuts, peppermint, raspberries, blackberries, loganberries, sweet cherries, pears, cauliflower, potatoes, and onions, just to name a few. Wheat is another very important crop.

In 2009, farmers and ranchers in Oregon took in $4.1 billion in sales. Crops accounted for 70 percent of these sales, with livestock, dairy products, and poultry responsible for the remaining 30 percent. In 2009, sales of cattle alone totaled nearly $630 million, and sales of dairy products totaled $400 million. Cattle and dairy products are two of the top five agricultural commodities produced in the state. Greenhouse and nursery products, hay, and grass seed are the other three products in the top five. Oregon farmers are some of the most efficient farmers in the world. This means that they achieve high crop yields per acre of land planted.

RECIPE FOR BLACKBERRY AND HAZELNUT COOKIE BARS

Wild blackberries can be found throughout Oregon. Combine fresh or frozen blackberries with Oregon's state nut to make this delicious treat.

WHAT YOU NEED

For the bottom crust:

$1/_2$ cup (115 grams) butter, softened

1 tablespoon (15 g) sugar

$1 \ 1/_2$ cups (180 g) all-purpose flour

For the filling:

5 cups (900 g) fresh or frozen blackberries

$3/_4$ cup (85 g) all-purpose flour

$1 \ 3/_4$ cup (390 g) sugar

For the topping:

$1/_2$ cup (100 g) brown sugar, firmly packed

$1/_3$ cup (75 g) butter, cut into small pieces

$1/_2$ cup (60 g) flour

$1/_2$ cup (40 g) rolled oats

1 teaspoon (3 g) cinnamon

$1/_2$ cup (40 g) chopped hazelnuts

Have an adult help you preheat the oven to 350 °F (175 °C). While the oven is heating, mix together the three ingredients for the crust until everything is nicely blended. Then press the crust into the bottom of a lightly greased 9-inch by 13-inch (25-cm by 35-cm) baking pan.

Wash the blackberries before preparing the filling. In a bowl, using a spoon, combine the berries with the flour and sugar. Then pour the filling over the bottom crust and spread it around.

After the filling is prepared, mix the ingredients for the topping in another bowl. The topping will be crumbly. Sprinkle it on top of the blackberry filling so that all of the filling is covered.

Place the pan into the preheated oven, and bake for one hour. Have an adult help you remove the pan from the oven—it will be hot. Let the treat cool for about 15 minutes before you cut it into squares. Then enjoy the cookie bars with some cool milk or some hot chocolate.

TILLAMOOK CHEESE

In 1909, ten independent cheese producers in Tillamook County got together and formed an association. They wanted to make sure that they produced quality dairy products. Today, about 110 family-owned dairy farms are members of the cooperative group, which is called the Tillamook County Creamery Association. Tillamook cheese can be found at stores across the United States. Other products—such as butter, yogurt, and ice cream—can be found in the western states. One million people visit the group's visitors' center every year, learning how cheese is made and tasting free samples. There is also a dairy festival and parade every June.

Fish and Wildlife

Another major industry in Oregon is based on the abundant wildlife in the state. In particular, many businesses make a great deal of money from seafood. Some of these businesses include canneries, fish and tackle supply stores, restaurants, and commercial fishing boats. There are more than 62,000 miles (100,000 km) of fishing streams, over 1,700 lakes, and, of course, the long Pacific shoreline in Oregon. The fish in both inland and coastal waters not only provide food for Oregonians and people all over the world—they also provide fun for people who like to fish as a sport. Almost 700,000 people buy fishing licenses each year in Oregon. Salmon and trout are the most popular fish to catch.

People also come to Oregon to hunt. In all, almost 300,000 people—both residents and visitors—buy hunting licenses each year in the state. The animals that are hunted include deer, elk, pronghorn antelope, and bighorn sheep. Cougar and bear, as well as water fowl such as ducks and geese, are also hunted.

Minerals and Metals

Oregon's supplies of natural gas and various minerals has created a new and growing industry. The sale of sand and gravel, cement and lime, crushed rock and other building materials, and clay and pumice is yet another way Oregonians make a living. Oregon also has a supply of gold and gemstones, such as agates, obsidians, and sunstones. Aluminum and steel are made in Oregon.

Cement plants, such as this one in Weatherby, employ many Oregonians.

Products & Resources

Wheat

Wheat is Oregon's most valuable food crop. Most of it grows in the northeastern part of the state. About one million acres (400,000 ha) of wheat are planted in Oregon each year.

Christmas Trees

Oregon is the biggest producer of Christmas trees in the United States, selling more than 7 million of them in 2008. Some of the most popular types of Christmas trees are the Scotch (or Scots) pine, Douglas fir, and noble fir. It takes six to ten years for these trees to grow big enough to sell.

Seacoast and Lighthouses

The seacoast is one of Oregon's most popular tourist attractions. During a trip to the coast, many people enjoy visiting some of the historic lighthouses located there. One of the most beautiful is the old lighthouse at Heceta Head, which was built in 1894. The light at Heceta Head is one of the strongest on the coast. It shines 21 miles (34 km) out to sea to warn ships of the rocky shoreline.

Seafood

Oregonians are very protective of their salmon and other fish. Each year, schoolchildren take on the task of stamping the silhouette of a fish near street drainage pipes, reminding everyone in their neighborhood not to dump toxic wastes into the sewers. All sewers eventually flow into the rivers and streams, and things like car oil, insecticides, and even laundry detergents can make fish sick.

Hazelnuts

With Oregon's fertile soil, rain, and sun, the state provides the perfect environment in which to grow hazelnuts. Around 99 percent of the hazelnut crop in the United States is grown in the Willamette Valley. The first hazelnut tree in Oregon was planted in 1858. One amazing fact about the hazelnut—Oregon's state nut—is that a hazelnut tree can produce nuts for more than eighty years.

Tourism

There are fourteen national forests in Oregon. Most of them are located in the mountains and along the rivers. Residents and tourists enjoy many outdoor activities in these forests, including backpacking, fishing, kayaking, skiing, and camping, as well as bird and wildlife watching.

Technology

Another type of business that in recent decades has supplied money and jobs for Oregonians is the technology industry. Businesses in this industry manufacture computer software, microchips, and other computer-based products.

Hewlett-Packard, a company that makes computers and printers, began to do some of its manufacturing in Oregon in the 1970s. The company has a large facility in Corvallis. Intel, another technology company, has seven centers in Oregon and is now the largest private employer in the state. A division of Symantec—which makes computer programs and provides other computer-related services—has offices in Eugene.

Services and Tourism

The service industry takes in more money than any other industry in Oregon. This industry includes businesses such as insurance companies, department stores and other retail stores, hospitals and health-care companies, law firms, real estate businesses, banks, and schools and colleges. Transportation is also considered part of the service industry, along with television stations and telephone companies.

Businesses providing services for tourists are part of the service industry as well. Oregon's tourism industry—which includes hotels and restaurants, as well as tourist attractions such as aquariums, museums, casinos, and historic sites—took in more than $8 billion in 2010. Tourism is very important to Oregon's economy. When tourists come to the state, they not only spend money—they also provide jobs,

> **Quick Facts**
>
> **TRAIL BLAZERS**
>
> Basketball fans in Oregon follow the Portland Trail Blazers. The team joined the National Basketball Association in 1970 and, just seven years later, won the NBA championship. Since 1995, the Blazers have played in Portland's Rose Garden arena, which can seat more than 20,000 basketball fans.

Many people come to Oregon to enjoy the spectacular scenery.

STAYING FIT
Popular sports and outdoor activities in Oregon include snowboarding, sledding, snowmobiling, hiking, mountain biking, and in-line skating.

because someone has to serve them. Waiters at restaurants benefit from tourists, as well as people who own gas stations, rental shops, and other businesses.

Oregon is often considered one of the most beautiful states in the nation, with its sandy beaches on the Pacific Coast, its tall, snow-capped mountains in the interior, and its high deserts along the eastern border. The natural beauty draws Oregonians outside, rain or shine, and makes them feel proud to be living in a place where the trees grow tall, the rivers run clear, and many people greet one another with welcoming smiles.

State Flag & Seal

Oregon is the only state whose flag has a different design on the front and on the back. The flag is navy blue with gold lettering and designs. Blue and gold are the state colors. On the front of the flag (shown left) are the words "State of Oregon," which are printed above a gold-colored image of the state seal. Below the seal is the year Oregon was admitted as a state: 1859. On the reverse side of the flag is a golden image of the beaver, referring to Oregon's nickname the Beaver State. Oregon's state flag was adopted in 1925.

The state seal was adopted in 1857. The words "State of Oregon" are printed at the top, and the year of Oregon's statehood is printed at the bottom. In the seal itself, a bald eagle is shown with its wings spread wide. The eagle is sitting on top of a shield, which shows a picture of the sun setting over the Pacific Ocean. Mountains and forests represent the natural resources of Oregon. There is also a covered wagon, standing for the pioneers who came to Oregon. A plow, a sheaf of wheat, and a pickax stand for the state's early agricultural and mining industries. Two ships represent the victory of the United States over Britain in controlling the land that became Oregon. Around the bottom of the shield are thirty-three stars, representing Oregon's rank as the thirty-third state to be admitted to the Union.

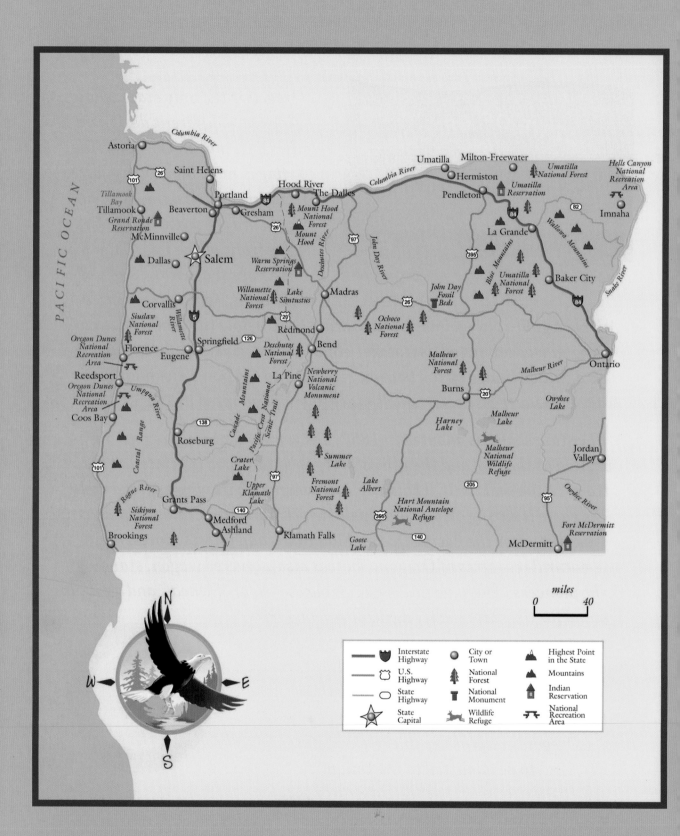

PACIFIC OCEAN

Columbia River

Astoria
Saint Helens
Tillamook Bay
Tillamook
Grand Ronde Reservation
McMinnville
Dallas
Portland
Beaverton
Gresham
Salem
Warm Springs Reservation
Willamette National Forest
Lake Simtustus
Mount Hood National Forest
Mount Hood
Deschutes River
Columbia River
Hood River
The Dalles
Umatilla
Milton-Freewater
Hermiston
Pendleton
Umatilla National Forest
Umatilla Reservation
Hells Canyon National Recreation Area
La Grande
Wallowa Mountains
Imnaha
Blue Mountains
Umatilla National Forest
Baker City
Snake River

Corvallis
Siuslaw National Forest
Willamette River
Springfield
Redmond
Bend
Madras
John Day River
John Day Fossil Beds
Ochoco National Forest

Oregon Dunes National Recreation Area
Florence
Eugene
La Pine
Newberry National Volcanic Monument
Malheur National Forest
Malheur River
Ontario

Reedsport
Oregon Dunes National Recreation Area
Coos Bay
Umpqua River
Coastal Range
Cascade Mountains
Pacific Crest National Scenic Trail
Burns
Harney Lake
Malheur Lake
Owyhee Lake

Roseburg
Summer Lake
Malheur National Wildlife Refuge
Jordan Valley

Crater Lake
Upper Klamath Lake
Fremont National Forest
Lake Albert
Owyhee River

Grants Pass
Rogue River
Siskiyou National Forest
Medford
Ashland
Klamath Falls
Goose Lake
Hart Mountain National Antelope Refuge
Fort McDermitt Reservation

Brookings
McDermitt

miles
0   40

N
W   E
S

Interstate Highway
U.S. Highway
State Highway
State Capital
City or Town
National Forest
National Monument
Wildlife Refuge
Highest Point in the State
Mountains
Indian Reservation
National Recreation Area

State Song

Oregon, My Oregon

words by John Andrew Buchanan
music by Henry B. Murtagh

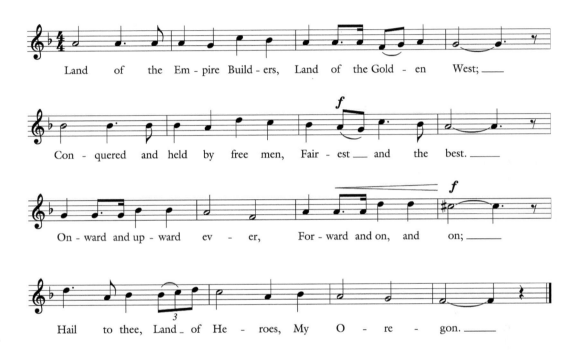

Land of the Em - pire Build - ers, Land of the Gold - en West;

Con - quered and held by free men, Fair - est and the best.

On - ward and up - ward ev - er, For - ward and on, and on;

Hail to thee, Land of He - roes, My O - re - gon.

BOOKS

Friedman, Mel. *The Oregon Trail*. New York: Children's Press, 2010.

Harness, Cheryl. *The Tragic Tale of Narcissa Whitman and a Faithful History of the Oregon Trail*. Washington, DC: National Geographic Society, 2006.

King, David C. *The Nez Perce*. New York: Marshall Cavendish Benchmark, 2008.

Ponte, June. *Fun and Simple Pacific West State Crafts: California, Oregon, Washington, Alaska, and Hawaii*. Berkeley Heights, NJ: Enslow Publishers, 2009.

WEBSITES

The Official Oregon State Website:
http://www.oregon.gov

State of Oregon Kids' Page:
http://oregon.gov/kids_korner.shtml

The Oregon Historical Society:
http://www.ohs.org

Visit Oregon:
http://www.traveloregon.com

Joyce Hart fell in love with writing while she was a student at the University of Oregon. She raised her children in Eugene and is currently a freelance writer and the author of six books. For the past twenty years she has enjoyed traveling the back roads of the Pacific Northwest.

Jacqueline Laks Gorman has been a writer and editor for approximately thirty years. She was raised in New York and moved to the Midwest in the 1990s. She and her family live in DeKalb, Illinois.

INDEX

Page numbers in **boldface** are illustrations.

INDEX